#SHOSPLE COLUPIS

WHEN THE SOCIAL NOTWORKS

TO IPAN

This series of illustrations intend to be a testimony of the social network time we are living through.

Show this thread

Sign up

Simon says

Find Friends

Log in

freakshow

User/loser/abusername or E-mail

Password

Log In

Forgot Password? 😆

Settings

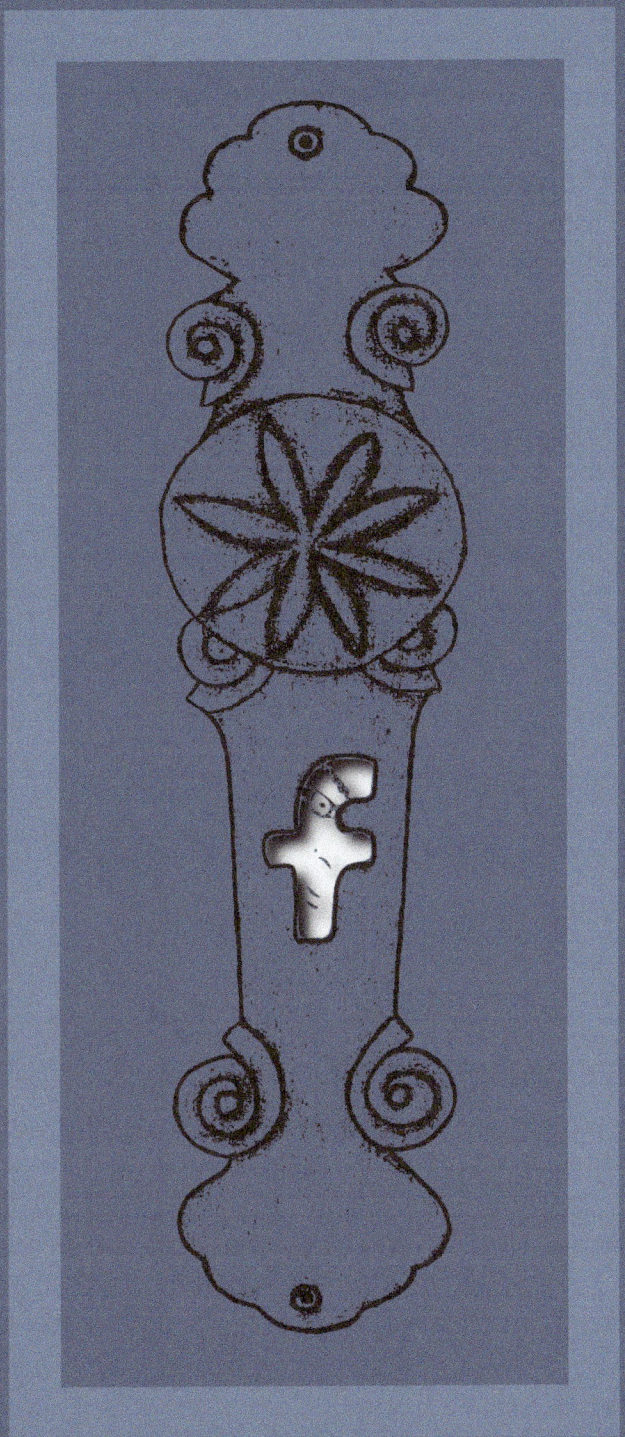

Profile Picture

Feed

What's on your mind?

What's on your mind?

What's on your mind?

What's on your mind?

What's on your mind?

MYA

What's on your mind?

What's on your mind?

#happiness#givememore

What...

WHAT RULES THE WORLD

IN 2019

Monkey see, monkey do

#brainfreeze

Monkey do not see, but monkey want to believe

A friend has commented (on) your status

ANOTHER SWELLED HEAD

Find Friends

Find Friends

Find Friends

Find Friends

unfriend

friend

friend friend

unfriend

unfriend

BLOCKED

BLOCKED

BLOCKED

FILTER
Ifriendyou IFRIENDYOUNOT

MIA

Find Friends

RELATIONSHIPS

MIA

Messages

f + password + you

= f + ***** U

SOCIAL

DISTANCING

Log out

Deactivate Account

Delete Account

Tschüss!

Refresh

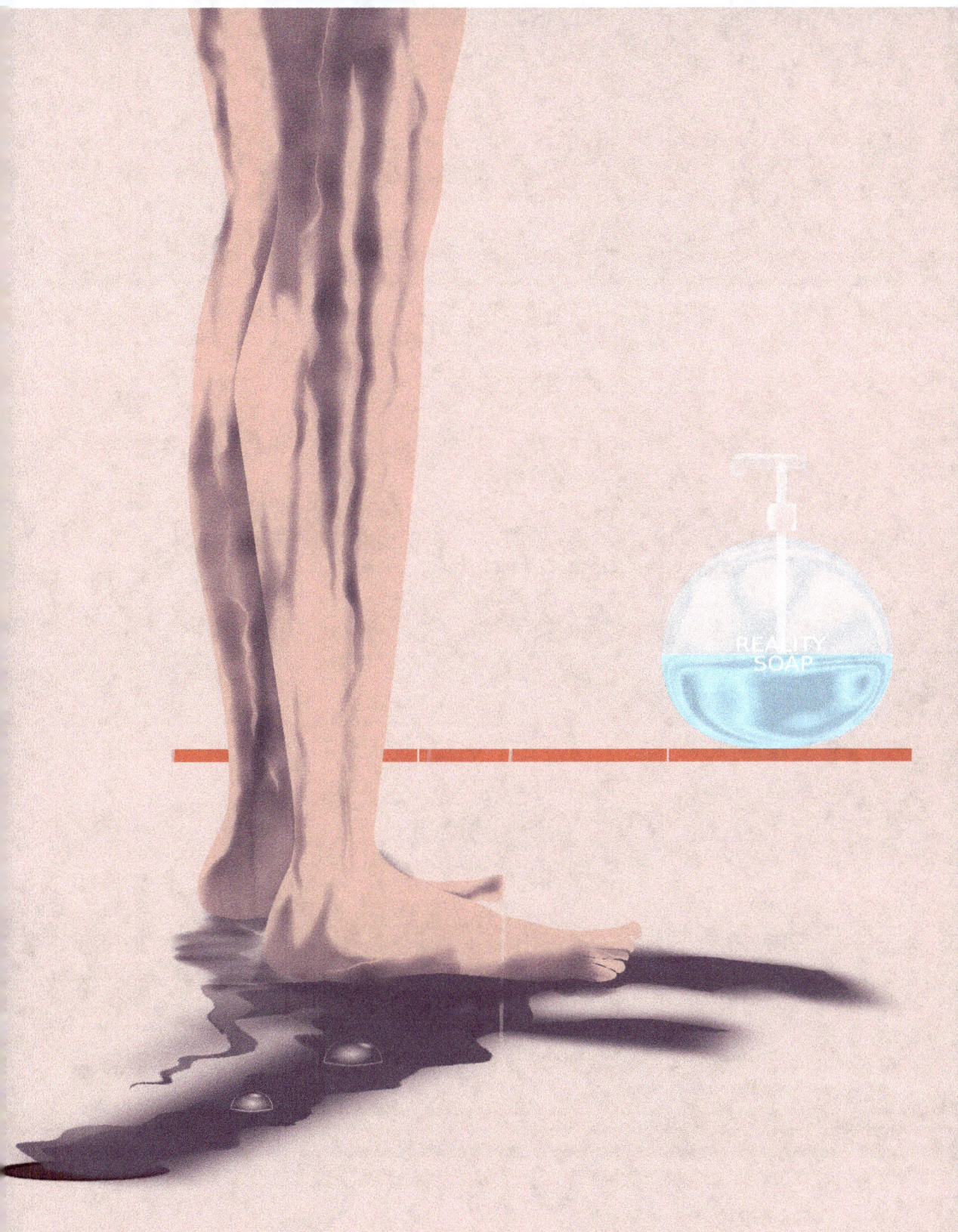

#CLEANSING

Home